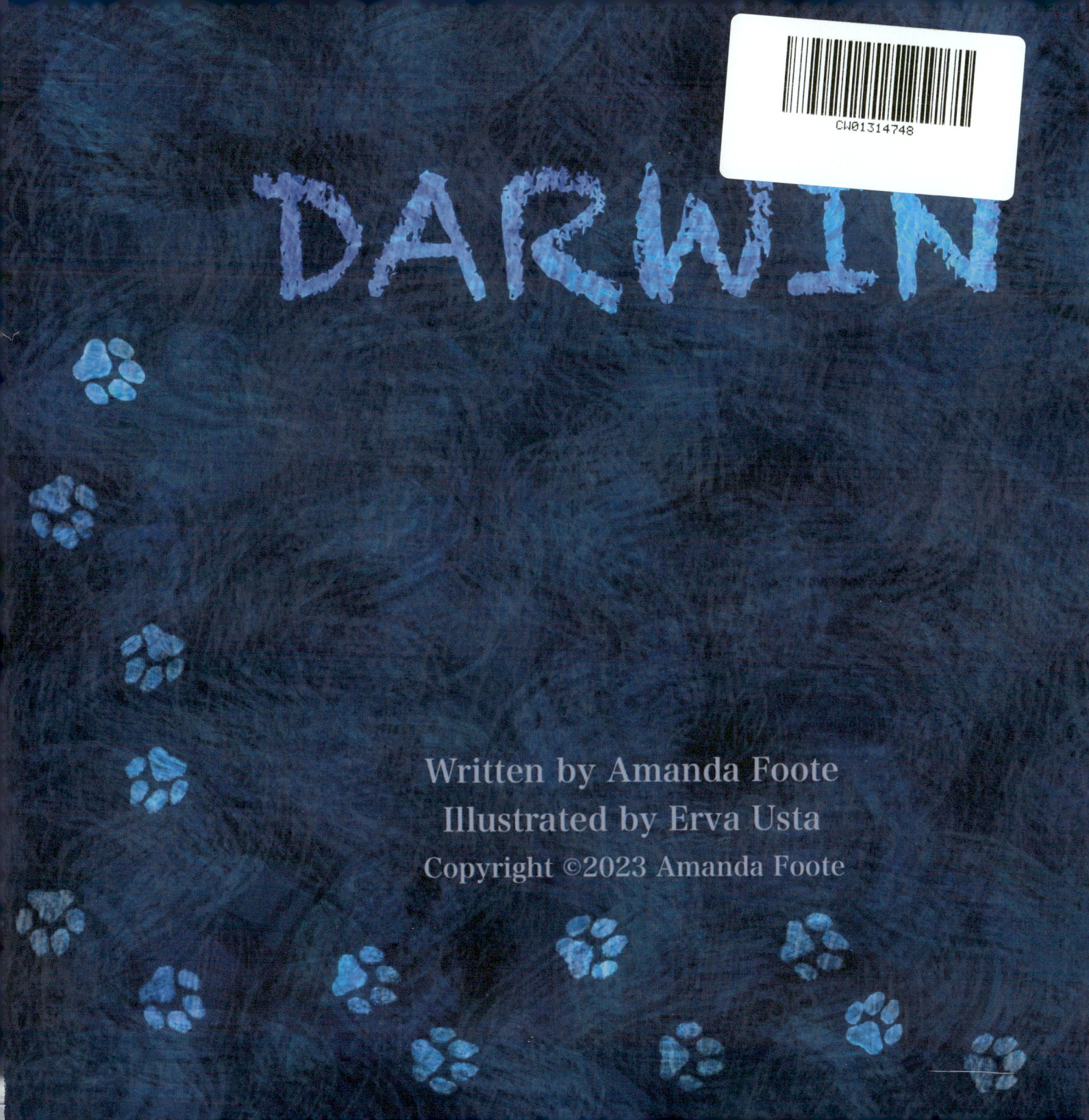

DARWIN

Written by Amanda Foote
Illustrated by Erva Usta
Copyright ©2023 Amanda Foote

Meet Mr Darwin, the hairy land shark.

His adventure began on a warm summer's day.
Stretching in bed and ready to play.

Out of one eye, he spotted a cat.

till he met a rat.

The little rat smiled and said,
"Come play with me in my garden shed!"

With that Darwin followed the rat and on the way they had a chat.

Along the road the excited pair sped.
Slightly ahead, the speedy rat led.

When they arrived, Darwin barked in delight.
For there lay a thrilling and glorious sight.

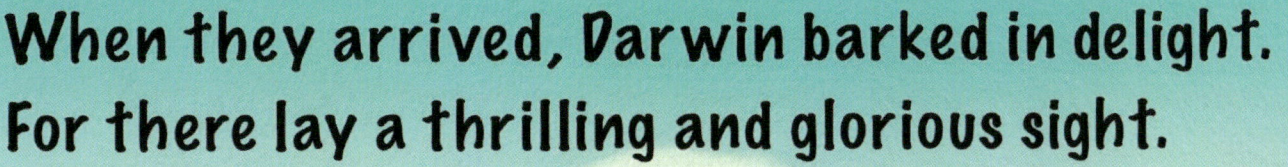

A can... Not any old can but a watering can.

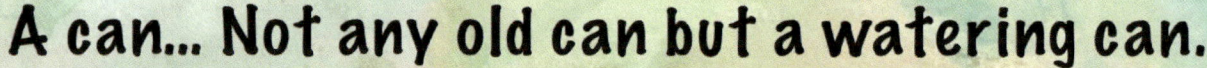

And that's when all the fun began!

In all his excitement, the zoomies began whilst he ran and he ran with his watering can.

his legs moved so fast it gave him a fright!

He dashed back and forth with the can in his grip,

After a while Darwin slumped by a Gnome.
The little rat said, "It's time to go home."

And with that, Darwin bid him goodbye to return to his home for a little shuteye.

Now, the adventure must come to an end. For our tired little pup has a bed to attend!

For Abi & Tom

Printed in Great Britain
by Amazon